Management: Q Prime Inc.

Transcribed by Jeff Jacobson

Cover artwork by Andres Serrano
Photography by Anton Corbijn

For a comprehensive listing of Cherry Lane Music's songbooks, sheet music, instructional materials, videos
and more, check out our entire catalog on the Internet. Our home page address is: http://www.cherrylane.com

CONTENTS

FULL COLOR FOLD-OUT

follows page 32

METALLICA... The Interview

by Steffan Chirazi

(Following are excerpts from "On The Couch With Dr. C." from So What!, the Metallica Club Magazine, Volume 3-Issue 1)

Not so long ago, I realized that cne of the few things Metallica had never done was allow themselves to be sat down and interviewed together for a couple of hours. There may have been the odd fortuitous situation where a journalist came across them all in a room, but one would always sneak away. I put this to drummer Lars Ulrich, and he agreed that, yes, it hadn't ever been done properly before. I asked him what he thought would happen if it were done now, and he said he could see it ending up as a wise-ass session. I disagreed. He thought some more about it. Put it to the others in the band. And here they are—Lars, guitarist/vocalist James Hetfield, guitarist Kirk Hammett, bassist Jason Newsted—all four band members at once—discussing band chemistry, growth and the evolution of the new album, **Load.**

It seems that sometimes you spend a lot of time separate from each other, particularly in recording situations.

LARS: I think we've spent more time together on this album then we have on any other before. It used to be me and James doing a lot of stuff—just the two of us—and we started opening up a lot more to the group thing with [producer] Bob Rock the last time. He thought what was missing on the ...*And Justice* thing was a group sound, a group vibe that we had live. So he started talking to us about trying to capture that in the studio. We started on it with the last record, and we've really honed in on it with this one. This is the most time we've ever spent together on a record.

JASON: When we all played together this time to record Lars's drum tracks, it was leaps and bounds more comfortable and more fun and productive than it was on the last record. The last record was kinda weird doing that with his drums, being in L.A. and everything, but this time when we did it with him it worked out to be good for everybody and especially best for him, the vibe of everybody being there knowing what was at stake, being more serious. Taking care of business, really, much better.

KIRK: And tons of vibe. You could feel it tracking off the floor when we were tracking certain songs, and it felt so great!

LARS: There's actually stuff of what you heard where there's the whole band off the floor. I mean off the floor! If you'd said that to us six months ago or five years ago, that would've been unheard of. Bob has pushed and pushed for that group Metallica thing to come across, and I think we're finally 100 percent comfortable with it. One can say, 'Why did it take so long?' and whatever, but it's just a natural evolvement process and it works!

JASON: The studio thing has definitely gotten more comfortable and I think since everybody has their own life, separate life that's really strong in its own way with their own set of friends, I think we're really comfortable when we do get together and do things like this.

You've led me into dealing with the differences in each other. It seemed to me when you were in the middle of doing the last record in L.A., that it was nearly impossible for you all to be in the same room at the same time. Right or wrong—was that the toughest time? Talk about looking at each other as individuals and saying, 'Alright, I can deal with him.' When did that start to happen more?

JASON: When we grew up, being able to have patience with each other.

JAMES: Getting away from each other helped us grow not apart but in our own ways, and then when we got back together we learned new ways of growing together. And I think that has happened in the studio as well. Lars was always, 'I have to record my drums this way.' I was, 'I have to record my vocals this way'—guitar and bass even. We were always kinda really stuck in one way. And we've kinda seen from each other how each person records his own way as well, and it's loosened up a lot.

LARS: I think what happened, in the year we took off, is we got a chance to hang out in our own worlds more, so as you're not always living in the shadow or presence of the other guy. It was always, 'Well, how am I dressed? What's James going to think? What's Kirk going to think?' Do you know what I mean? You're always playing off each other, so when you spend a year off from each other and suddenly come back like we did for the summer '94 tour, everybody was a lot more comfortable and confident with their own selves. And that brought a lot to the table.

JASON: Since I joined the band, that was the first time anybody got to go away and enjoy the fruits of the labor and all that kind of thing. That was the first time anybody got to go and be themselves and truly enjoy doing it. Whether it was gun stuff or scuba stuff or whatever stuff.

KIRK: I think we came to a point where our confidence grew both personally and with each other. We got more independent, but within the context of our relationship together things got stronger.

For many years, probably right up to the 'Black' album, it seemed to be an iron-clad band philosophy of 'It must be seen as the four.' When was it decided to come out and be open about how it is, that there's basically the main nucleus of Lars and James, with Jason and Kirk coming in with ideas. How easy was that for you (Kirk and Jason) to acknowledge?

KIRK: It's always never been easy for me because it's... never been easy. A lot of the time these guys had such a strong vision that it was hard for them to stray a little bit this way or that way. But nowadays, like I said, they're much more open-minded and it makes a really big difference in the old 'vibe' sense. It's better this way because we feed off each other a lot more having the same vibe.

Has it been easier not having to keep up this iron-clad 'four-as-one' image?

JAMES: That's just confidence within each other and within ourselves.

LARS: We're a lot more open about whatever goes on with us. Me and [James] had a very narrow vision; [now] we're more open and trying new things and moves musically and attitude-wise. And there's so many things not just within but around us that have changed. Look around.

You're talking about success.

LARS: No, no—more about the musical climate and people's attitudes, and how to deal with it. There was very much a time maybe five years ago where it was 'Metallica.' This is what Metallica is and this is what Metallica should be, and I think it keeps sort of expanding. I think we're a lot less locked into what Metallica should be. If anything, to me, Metallica is about blossoming, growing....

JAMES: Evolving even more....

KIRK: And I think a lot of it has to do with Bob Rock, and his attitude at the beginning of the record. He came up to me and said, 'Y'know, you and Jason are going to have a lot more to do on this album than before,' and I think in a very subtle way he opened that up and planted the seed with [Lars and James].

LARS: The seed was planted on the last record, but it just took five years to get fully comfortable with it.

JAMES: About this whole word of 'looseness' on the record. It didn't really come into play, I think, until a bit later, when we were all kinda sittin' and jammin' together. One thing for me was that I went on this hunting trip for a couple of weeks and, hahaha, soon as I came back there was this tape. And it was like, 'Alriiiight, we did a few things,' and there's this tap dancing in the background—'a few things we experimented with.' Yeah? Okay, what is it? 'Well, Lars was joking around, doing some singing....' Oh, yeah, funny, haha. 'There's this other thing.... Kirk played rhythm guitar.' WHAAAAT!!! So I listened to the stuff, and it was pretty f***in' cool. We've got two guitar players, so use two guitar players.

LARS: This happened about a week later! *(laughter)*

JAMES: Yeah, well, it took a little time. It's all about conditioning.

You're conditioned to do something one way for 15 years, and then all of the sudden it changes. 'Whoooooaaaaa, hold it! Troubling!'

LARS: Especially when it changes in a place where he's three days from the nearest phone. He comes back, and to this day he thinks we had it planned....

KIRK: I was afraid he was going to hit me. (*laughs*)

LARS: But it's a perfect example of adapting and of Bob trying to make it more of a band.

JAMES: Deep down I always had this feeling of 'Kirk's the amazing lead guitar player and I'm the rhythm guitar player.' But with him experimenting with new sounds in the studio, different stuff while we're tracking, 'Wow, is that how bands record?' We've discovered a whole new way of recording.

LARS: One of the most interesting things is, that in terms of basic guitar riff and basic guitar ideas, this is probably the most Kirk has ever contributed to a Metallica album.

KIRK: Even in the songwriting thing, I've contributed.

It seems to me Kirk seems to glide his way through things without butting heads with anyone.

KIRK: Well....

JAMES: Look how smooth he is!

KIRK: It all makes sense to me in the end. A lot of their decisions make sense to me initially. I'm thinking the same thing; it's just that many times Lars has beaten me to the punch.

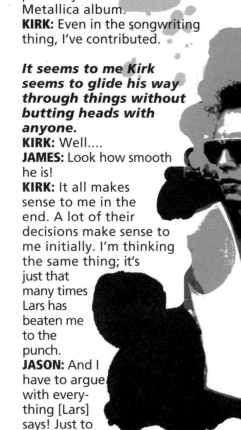

JASON: And I have to argue with everything [Lars] says! Just to make sure he's right. See, he thinks I argue with him just because it's him....

LARS: And I will think that until the day I die! (*laughter*)

JASON: Now a percentage of that, perhaps, is true....

LARS: Like 'high '90s'!

JASON: But a lot of the time I argue so as to stir shit up, so as we can make sure that we know and have checked on the shit. Usually he has it covered, anyway.

LARS: I'm not getting into too many details right now, but there really is a vibe of 'experiment' and of the unit standing together and trying different things musically and attitude-wise. We did some photo stuff a couple of weeks ago, and without getting more into it we did some stuff that we'd never tried before. And I walked away from that session feeling we were a stronger unit because we went for it at the same time. Musically, the hardest thing is going to be to curb all the experimenting because we have to finish this record in a couple of months. Instead of five years ago, when it was like 'Oh, well, let's try this,' now it's a case of not getting so out of hand, of contain-

ing the desire to experiment. That spirit in the ranks has really brought us closer together than ever before.

KIRK: I think we're at our fullest potential now than ever before. The sky's the f***ing limit.

LARS: All preconceived and preexisting ideas of who we are and what we've done are at a point right now where we're standing at a massive potential point of rebirth.

Interesting you should see it that way, when so many people who get to that position see themselves as standing at the edge of a precipice waiting to fall off and die.

JAMES: Yeah, 'It's the end.'

LARS: Every other time we made a record I always knew the end point before we started.

Even for the 'Black' album?

LARS: I knew the 12 songs we were going to record before we started. I knew what the record would look like, I knew what the record would more or less sound like. When we started this record last summer, there was still no cap on. We were still writing new songs in November; there's two songs on the album me and James wrote in f***ing November! Now you can see the end of it, but when we started it we had all these songs, all these ideas, that we knew there might be more songs and more ideas so we kept an open mind and tried shit. This is the first time I've been able to see the end of this record.

JASON: When we first started we were looking at a mass of 25 to 30 songs, 'Who knows, it's going to be three albums.' How could you see the end of that?! Finally, the stages we went through, the personal meetings, the seeing each other, meeting with management resulted in that many songs? You're going to do that many songs, take that many months and you'll have strangled each other. So what's it going to be?

LARS: After we started writing we got to 24 to 25 songs, and we said, 'This is crazy; we can carry on writing songs until the year 2007. Let's go in the studio and start recording.' The ideas for the songs were still lying there; we had to curb ourselves and put a lid on it because we could still be in there right now. That's how many ideas kept surfacing, so it really became an exercise in sitting down and figuring out what you wanted to do. But looking back, I think the last year has been great. The fact that we went and did those gigs did so much for us in terms of making the record, so many things have happened in the last year that have brought us to the moment we're at now. I don't think we would feel so good about what we're doing right now if it hadn't evolved like it has.

AIN'T MY BITCH

Words and Music by
James Hetfield and Lars Ulrich

9

*Vib. w/slide throughout solo.

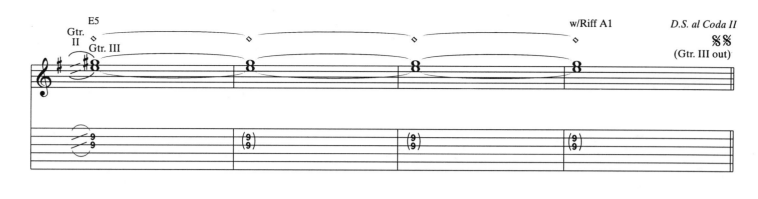

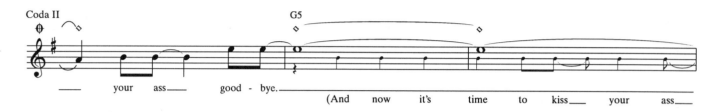

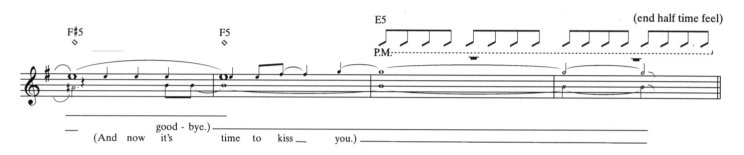

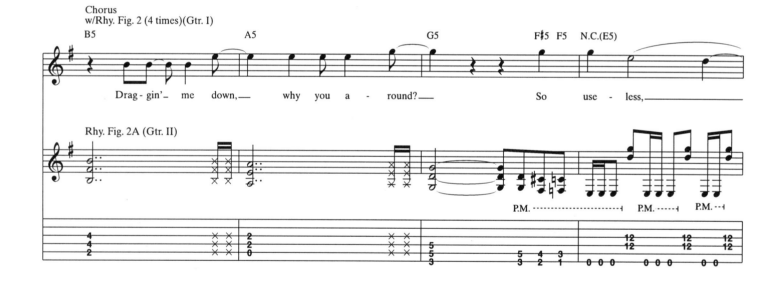

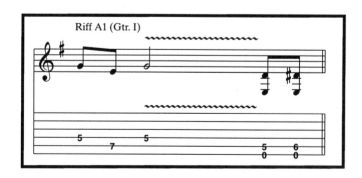

18

2 X 4

Words and Music by James Hetfield,
Lars Ulrich and Kirk Hammett

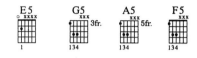

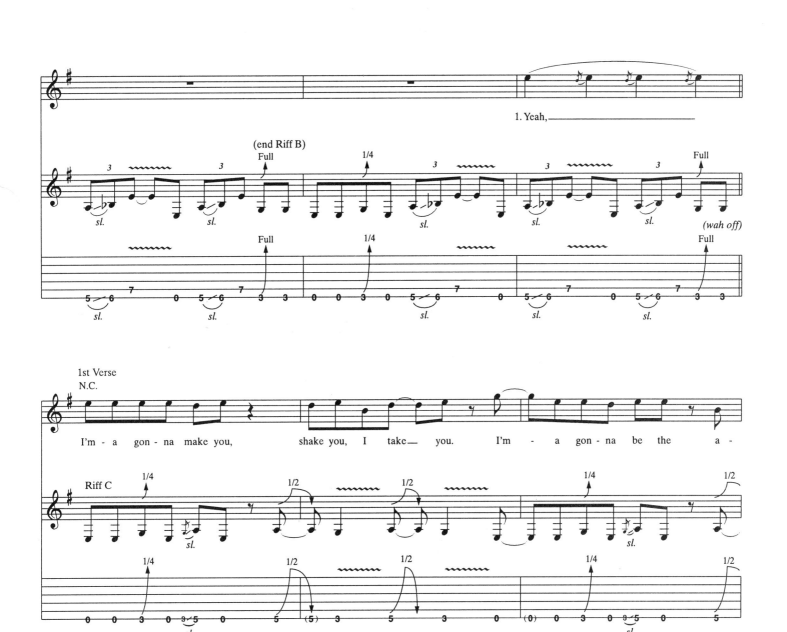

1. Yeah,

(end Riff B)
Full

1st Verse
N.C.

I'm - a gon - na make you, shake you, I take— you. I'm - a gon - na be the a -

Riff C

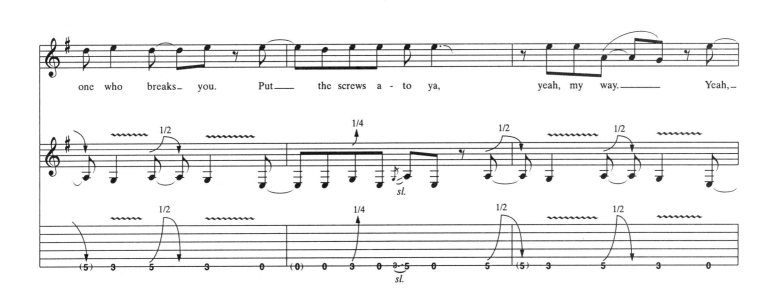

one who breaks— you. Put— the screws a - to ya, yeah, my way.— Yeah,—

come on - a come on, ___ come and make ___ my day, ___

(end Riff C)

*Gtr. II: w/wah as filter (next 4 bars only)

oh, ___ make my day. ___ 2. Yeah, ___ ya

2nd, 3rd Verses
w/Riff C
N.C.

got some hell to pay - a, I steal your thun - der. The joy ___ of vi - 'lent move - ment
3. See additional lyrics

w/Fill 1

pulls you un - der. Ooh, ___ bite the bul - let, well, hard. ___ Yeah, —

— but I die hard - er, so go ___ too far, ___

Fill 1 (Gtr. III)

w/wah as filter

too far.

Chorus
2nd time w/Fill 2
N.C.
Bkgd. Voc. Fig. 1

(Fric - tion, fu - sion, ret - ri -

*Gtr. I indicated to right of slashes in TAB.

Fill 2 (Gtr. III)

Play 8 times

mf w/wah as filter

(Gtr. III out)

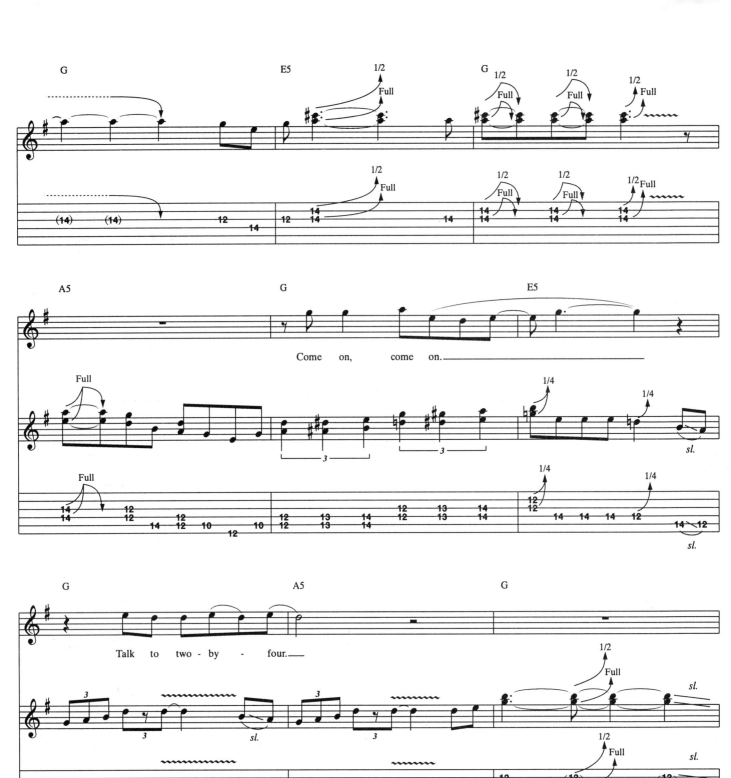

Come on, come on._____

Talk to two - by - four._____

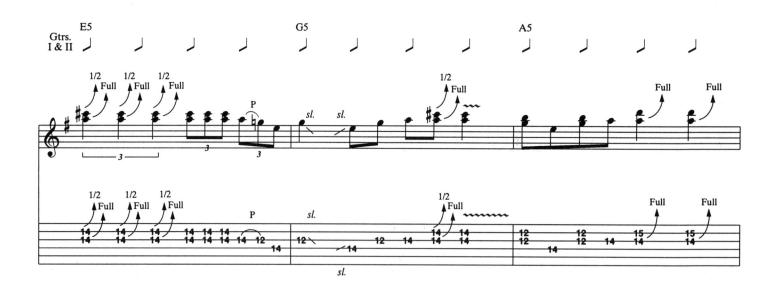

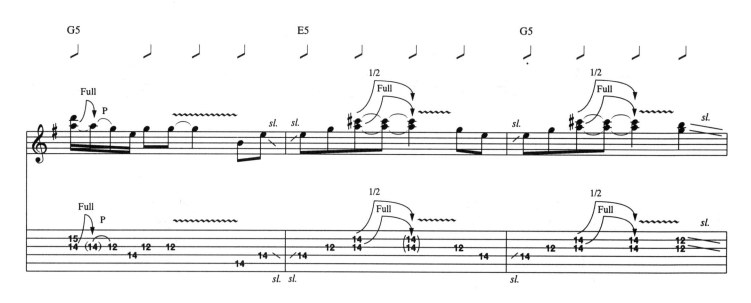

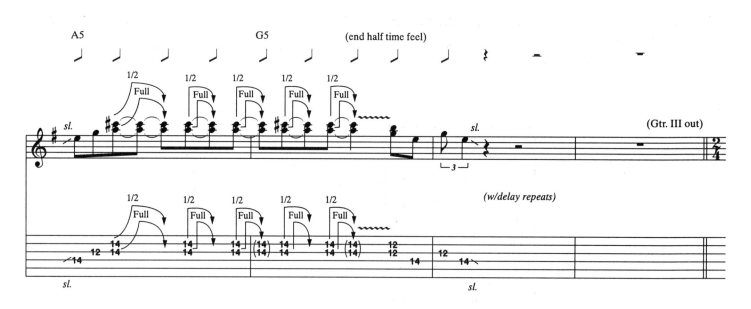

w/Riff A
N.C.

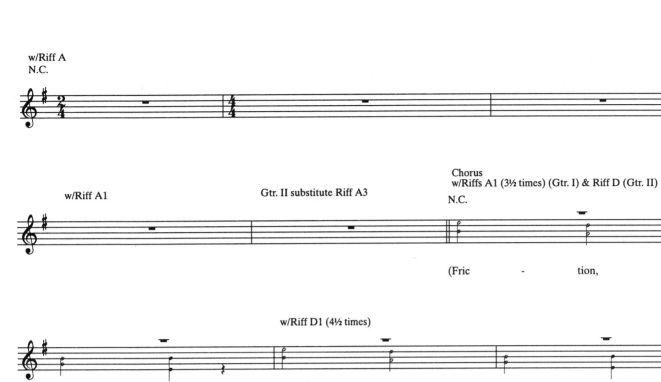

w/Riff A1   Gtr. II substitute Riff A3

Chorus
w/Riffs A1 (3½ times) (Gtr. I) & Riff D (Gtr. II)
N.C.

(Fric   -   tion,

w/Riff D1 (4½ times)

fu   -   sion,   ret   -   ri   -   bu   -   tion.)

w/Bkgd. Voc. Fig. 1 (2 times)

I'm gon - na make you_____ talk   to   me.   I'm gon - na take you,   ooh, ___

w/Riff A4   E5   w/Rhy. Fig. 1 (Gtr. I)   G5   A5

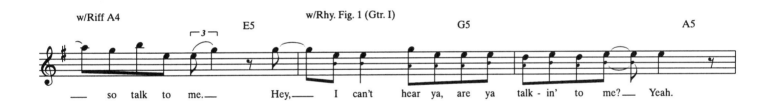

___ so talk to me. ___   Hey, ___ I can't hear ya, are ya talk - in' to me? ___ Yeah.

Riff A4 (Gtr. I)

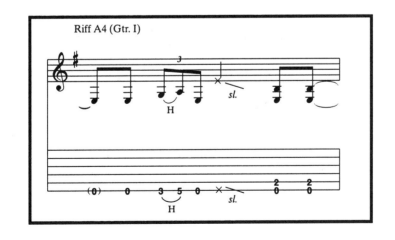

Additional Lyrics

3. Yeah, I'm gonna make you, shake you, take you.
   I'm gonna be that one who breaks you.
   Put the screws to ya my way.
   Hey, come on, come on,
   Come and make my day, make my day. *(To Chorus)*

THE HOUSE JACK BUILT

Words and Music by James Hetfield,
Lars Ulrich and Kirk Hammett

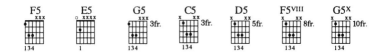

Tune down 1/2 step:

⑥=E♭ ③=G♭
⑤=A♭ ②=B♭
④=D♭ ①=E♭

Moderately slow Rock ♩ = 100

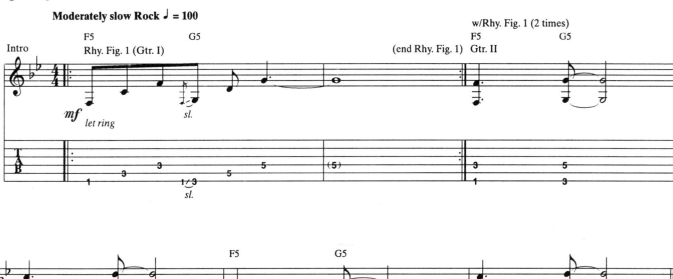

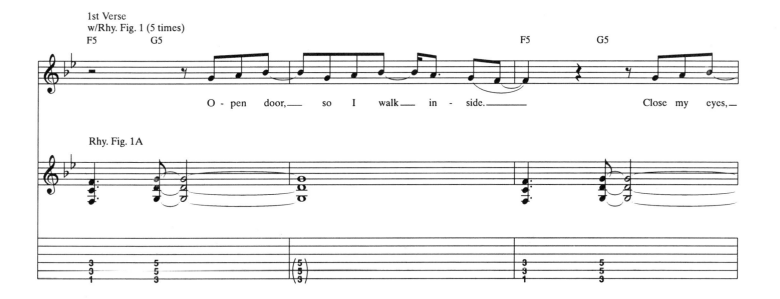

1st Verse
w/Rhy. Fig. 1 (5 times)

O - pen door, — so I walk — in - side. — Close my eyes, —

Rhy. Fig. 1A

33

find my place to hide. And I shake as I take it in.

w/Riff A

Let the show be gin.

(end Rhy. Fig. 1A)

Gtr. II

P.M.

(cont. in slashes)

Gtr. I

Riff B

P.M.

let ring

H P P

H P P

1/2

1/2

Riff A (Gtr. III)

(Gtr. III out)

mp

34

Is that the moon — or just a light that lights — this dead end —

*Riff C

sl.

sl.

*Two gtrs. arr. for one

w/Rhy. Fig. 3 (1st 3 bars only) and Riff C

N.C.

E(♭5)

— street?

(end Riff C)

Is that you there —

w/Rhy. Fill 1

(Gtr. III out)

N.C.

— or just an-oth-er de-mon that — I meet? — The

Chorus
F5   G5   C5   D5   F5 XIII   G5 X

Rhy. Fig. 4A
(Gtr. II)

high-er you are,   the   far-ther you fall.   The   long-er the walk,   the

Rhy. Fig. 4 (Gtr. I)

sl.

let ring

sl.

Swal - low me_____ so the pain____ sub - sides._____

Gtr. III

Full

Full

And I shake____ as I take____ the sin.____

Full

1/2

Full

1/2

Let the show____ be - gin.____

(Gtr. III out)

Full

sl.

Full

sl.

w/Rhy. Fig. 4 (1st 4 bars only) (Gtrs. I & II)
w/Bkgd. Voc. Fig. 2

The

Bkgd. Voc. Fig. 2

Let the show__ be - gin.____
Let the show__ be - gin.____

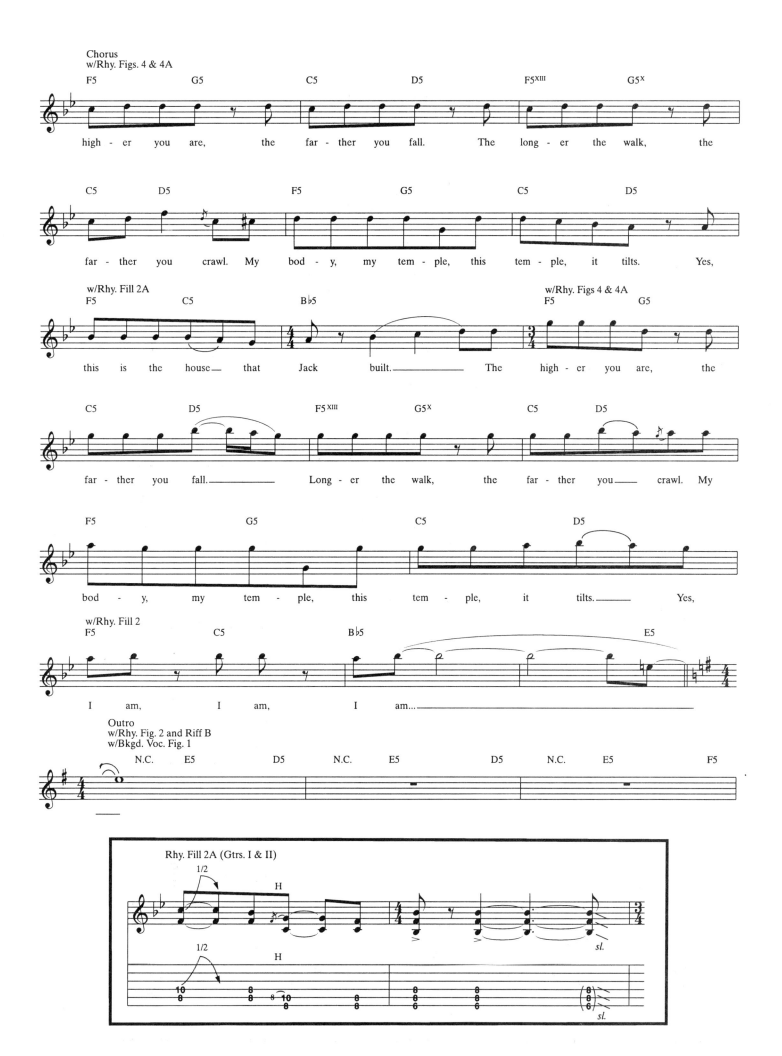

*Flick pickup selector back and forth ad lib (this bar only).

UNTIL IT SLEEPS

Words and Music by
James Hetfield and Lars Ulrich

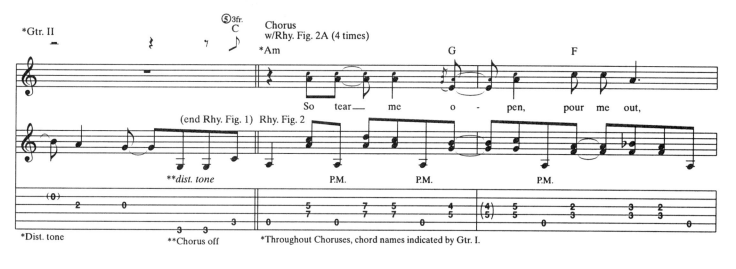

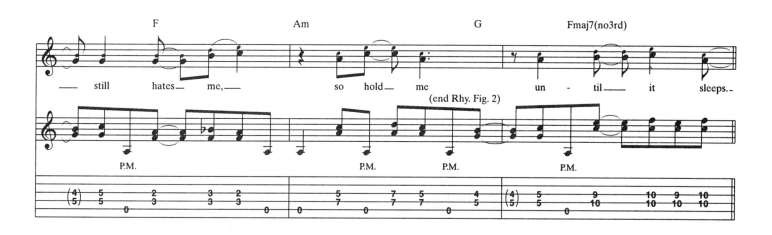

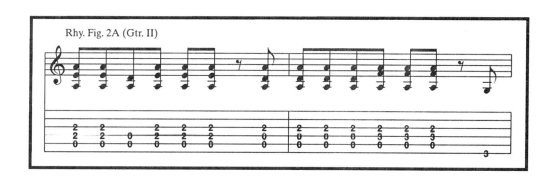

A5   G   Fsus2

Gtr. II

clean tone w/chorus
dim.   let ring

Rhy. Fig. 3 (Gtr. I)   (end Rhy. Fig. 3)

clean tone w/chorus
let ring

2nd Verse
w/Rhy. Fig. 1
*Am   N.C.

Just like —— the curse, —— just like the stray. ——

Gtr. II

let ring

*Throughout Verses, chord names indicated by Gtr. I.

Am

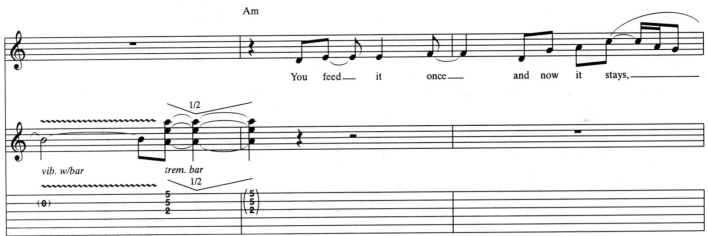

You feed —— it   once —— and now it stays, ——

vib. w/bar   trem. bar
                 1/2

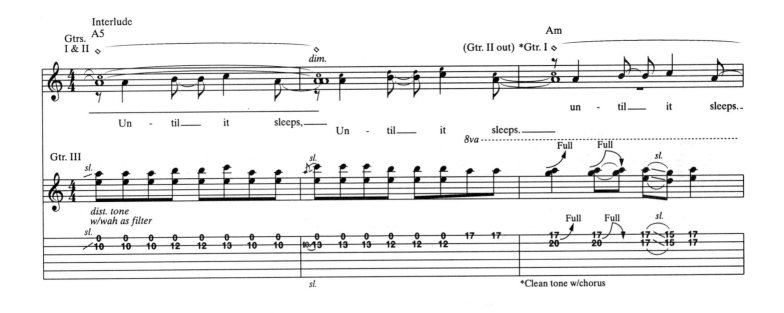

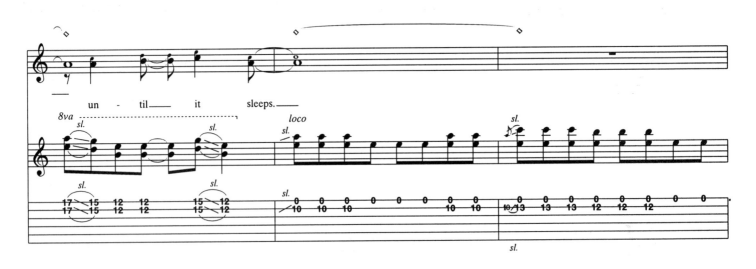

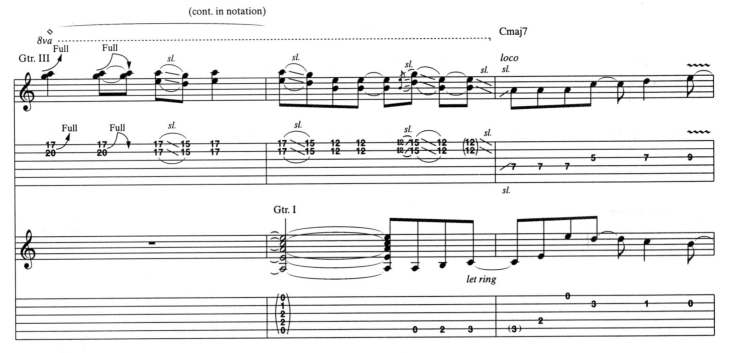

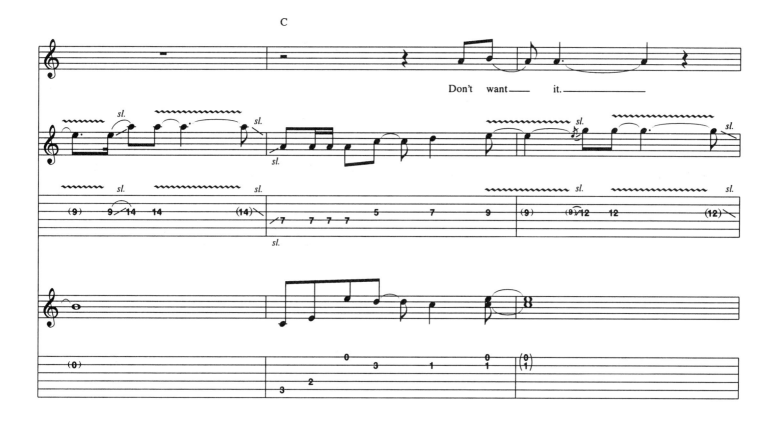

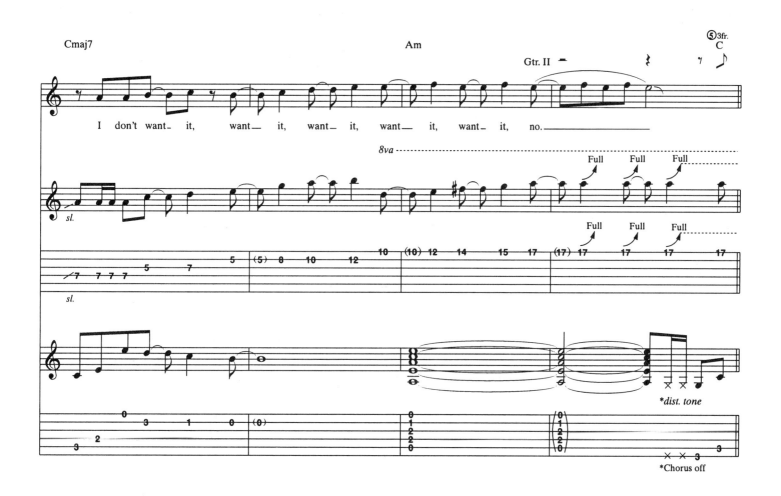

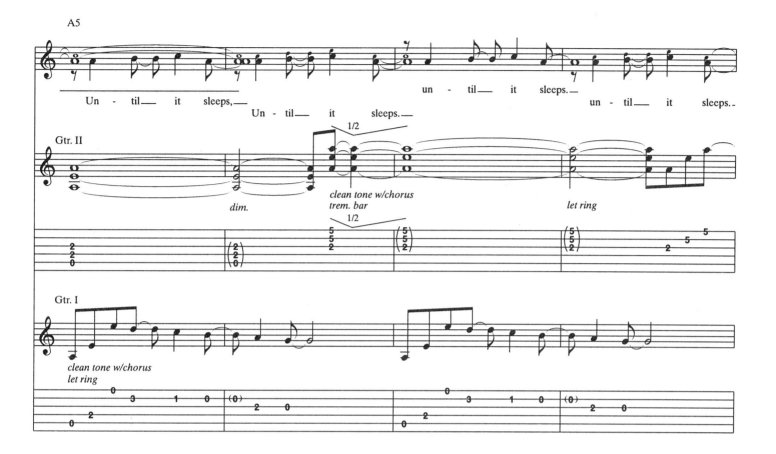

Un - til — it sleeps, — un - til — it sleeps. — un - til — it sleeps. —

Un - til — it sleeps. —

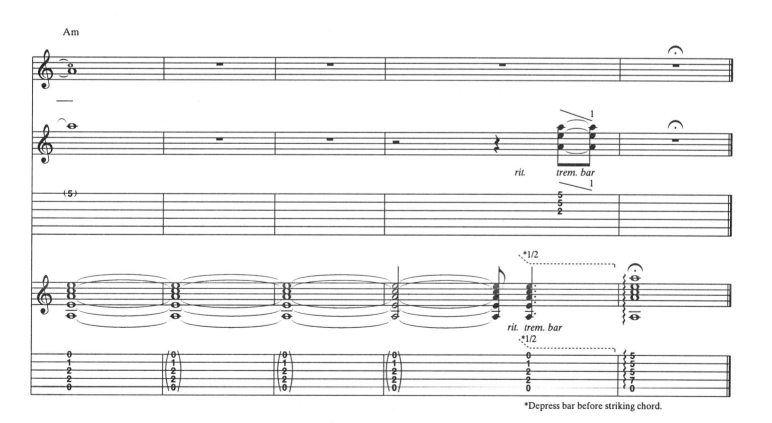

*Depress bar before striking chord.

KING NOTHING

Words and Music by James Hetfield,
Lars Ulrich and Kirk Hammett

Half time feel
Pre-chorus

N.C.(A5)

You dig to make your name.
You wish your life a-way.

Are you pac-i-fied?

All the wants you waste, all the things

Rhy. Fig. 3

(end Rhy. Fig. 3)

w/Rhy. Fig. 3 (Gtr. II)

Eb5   N.C.(A5)

Rhy. Fill 2 (Gtr. I)

Full

(end half time feel) Chorus

Eb5   E5
*Gtr. II

— you've changed.

Then it all crash-es down, and you break your crown.

*2nd & 3rd times, Gtr. II plays w/rhythmic variations ad lib (next 7 bars only).
**Substitute upstem note on D.S.

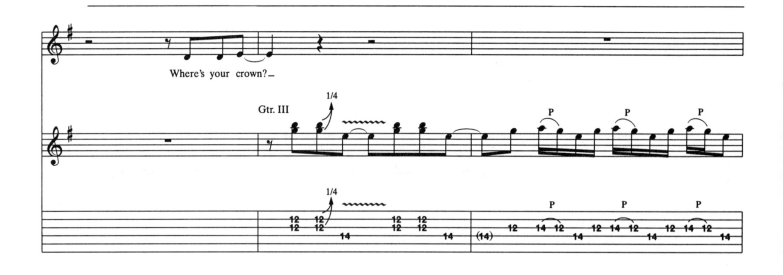

Where's your crown?

Gtr. III

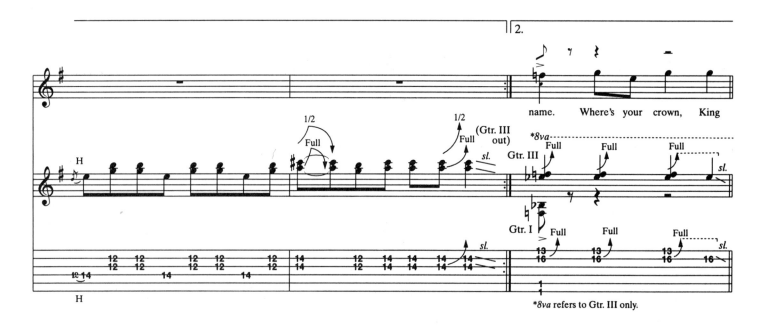

name. Where's your crown, King

*8va refers to Gtr. III only.

Guitar solo
w/Rhy. Fig. 1 (4 times) (Gtrs. I & II)
N.C.(E5)

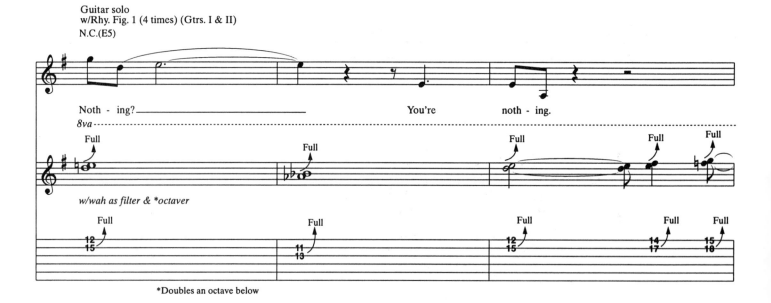

Noth - ing? You're noth - ing.

8va

w/wah as filter & *octaver

*Doubles an octave below

Come on,— where's your crown?

w/Rhy. Fig. 3 (1½ times)
(A5)

Gtr. I substitute Rhy. Fill 2
N.C.(A5)

w/Rhy. Fill 3
Eb5

Eb5

(Vocal: Huh!)

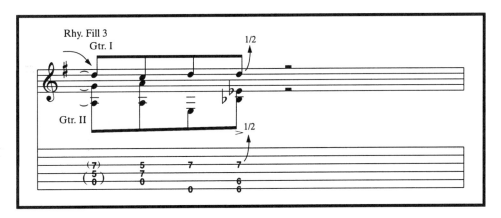

Rhy. Fill 3
Gtr. I

Gtr. II

you say. Care - ful what you— wish,— you— may— re - gret— it. Care - ful

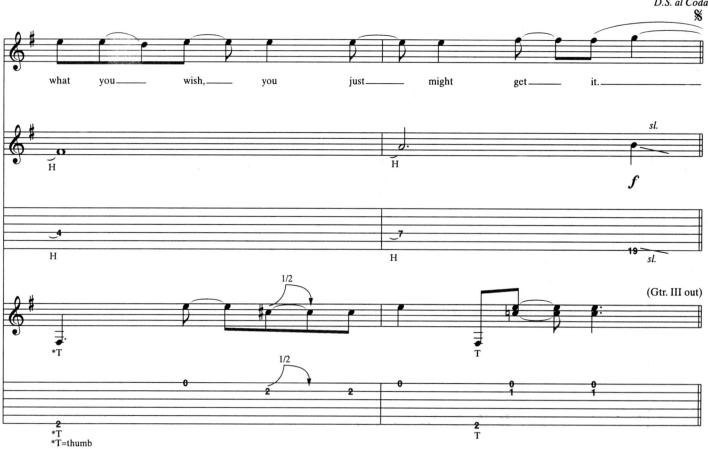

what you— wish,— you just— might get— it.—

*T=thumb

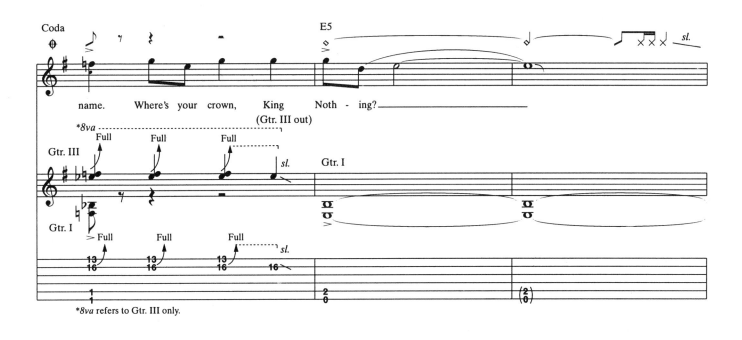

name. Where's your crown, King   Noth - ing?

*8va refers to Gtr. III only.

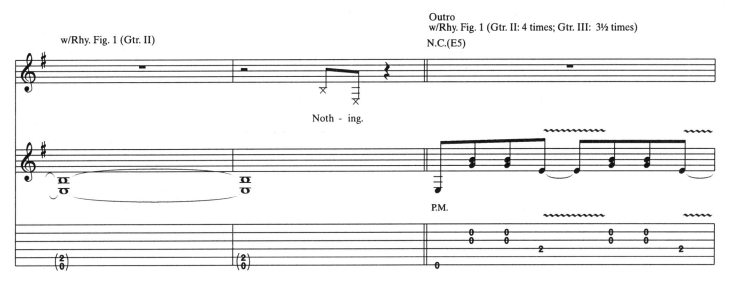

Noth - ing.

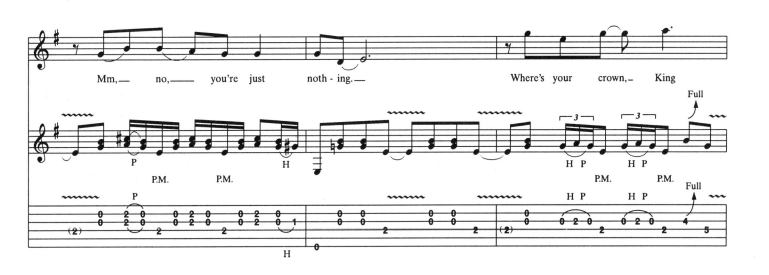

Mm, ___ no, ___ you're just ___ noth - ing. ___ Where's your crown, ___ King

Noth - ing?___   No,_____ you're just   noth - ing.___

w/Rhy. Fill 5

Free time
E5
Gtrs. I & II

Ab - so - lute - ly   noth - ing.
(cont. in slashes)

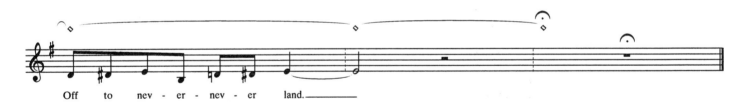

Off   to   nev - er - nev - er   land.___

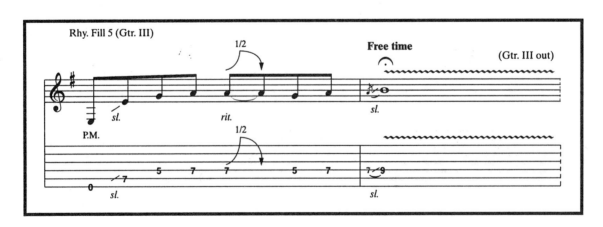

Rhy. Fill 5 (Gtr. III)

1/2

Free time

(Gtr. III out)

HERO OF THE DAY

Words and Music by James Hetfield,
Lars Ulrich and Kirk Hammett

Tune down 1/2 step:

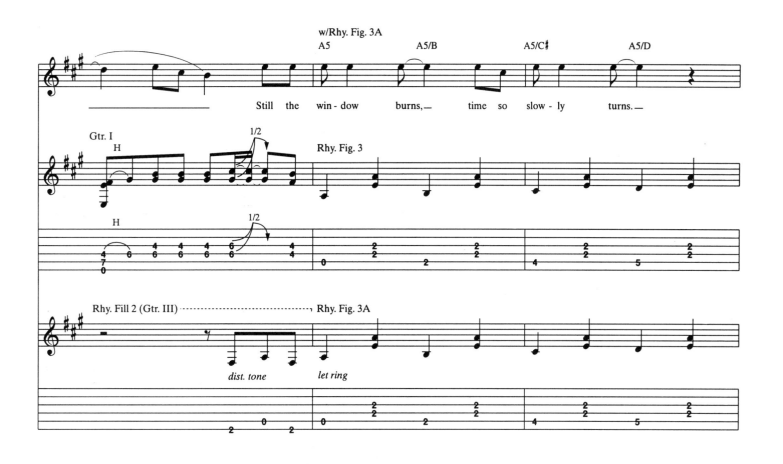

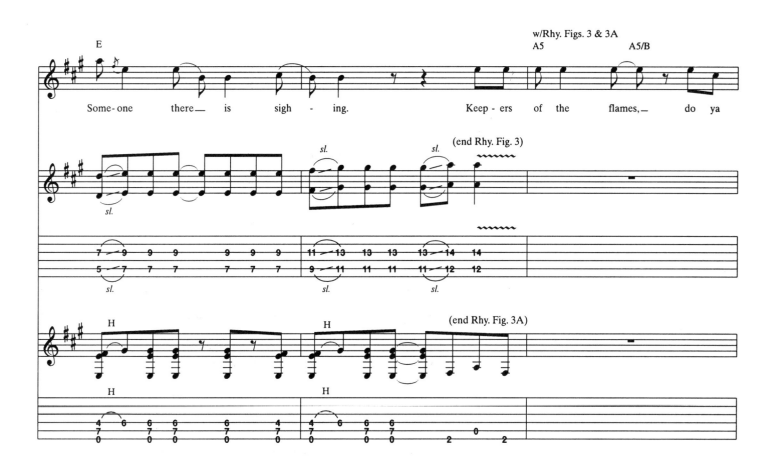

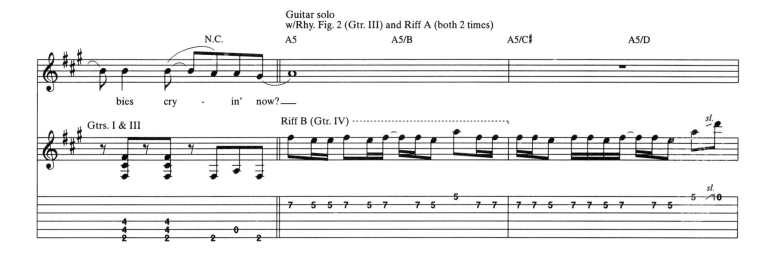

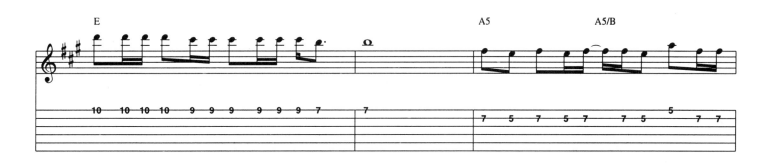

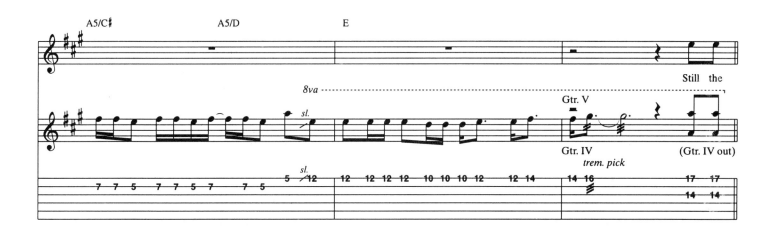

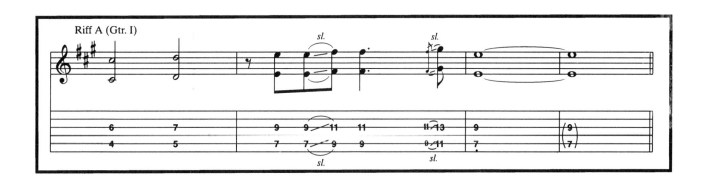

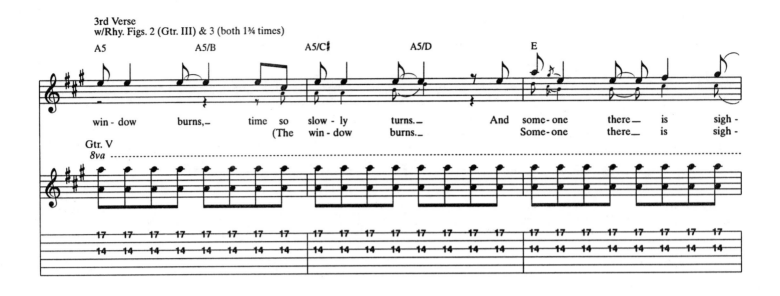

3rd Verse
w/Rhy. Figs. 2 (Gtr. III) & 3 (both 1¾ times)

win - dow   burns,—   time so   slow - ly   turns.—   And   some - one   there— is   sigh -
(The   win - dow   burns.—   Some - one   there— is   sigh -

Gtr. V

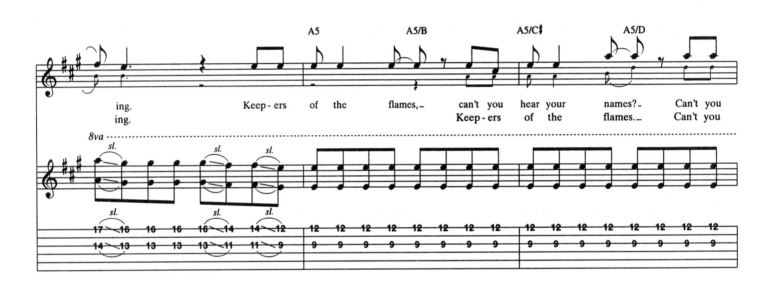

ing.   Keep - ers   of the   flames,—   can't you   hear your   names?—   Can't you
ing.   Keep - ers   of the   flames.—   Can't you

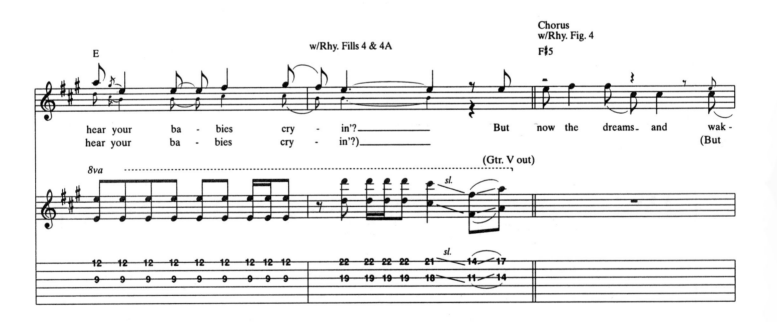

hear your   ba - bies   cry - in'?——————   But   now the   dreams— and   wak -
hear your   ba - bies   cry - in'?)   (But

w/Rhy. Fills 4 & 4A

Chorus
w/Rhy. Fig. 4

(Gtr. V out)

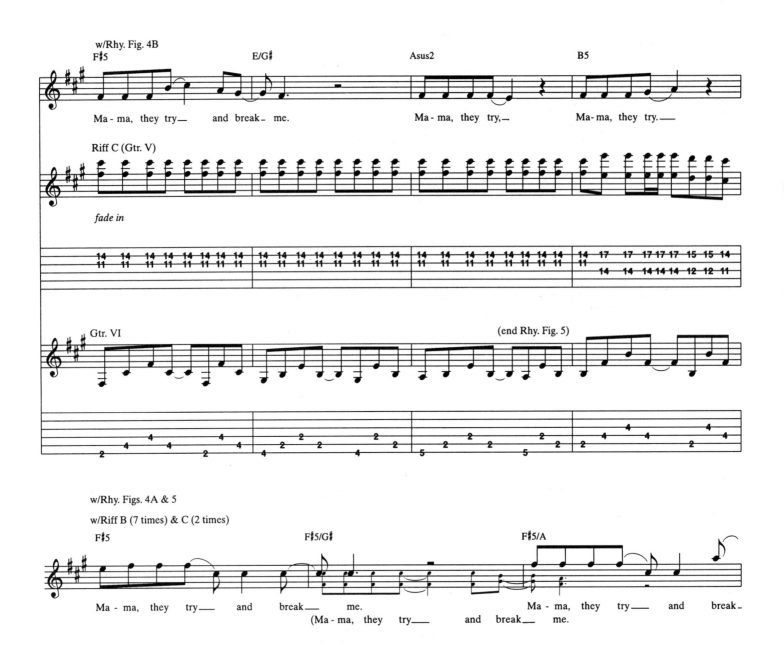

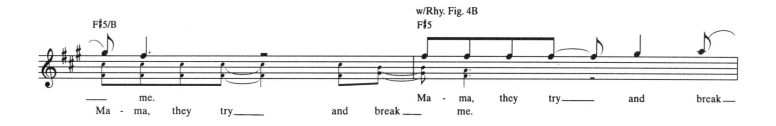

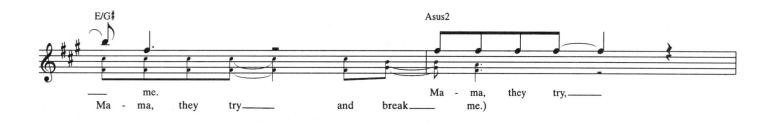

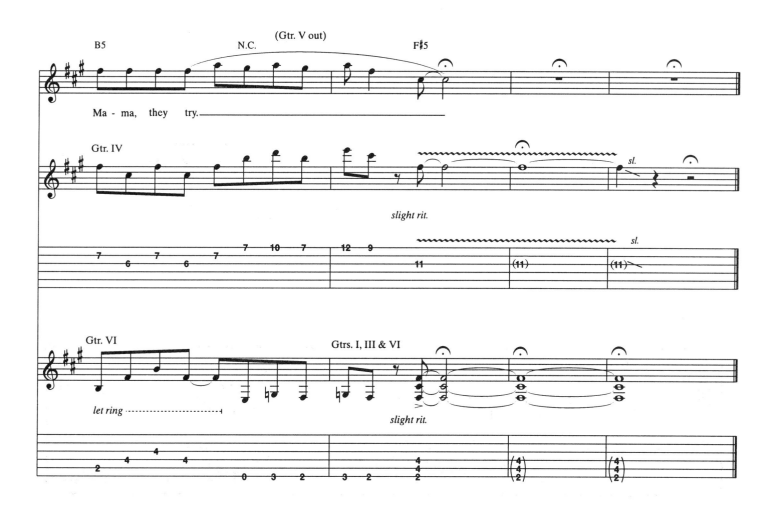

BLEEDING ME

Words and Music by James Hetfield,
Lars Ulrich and Kirk Hammett

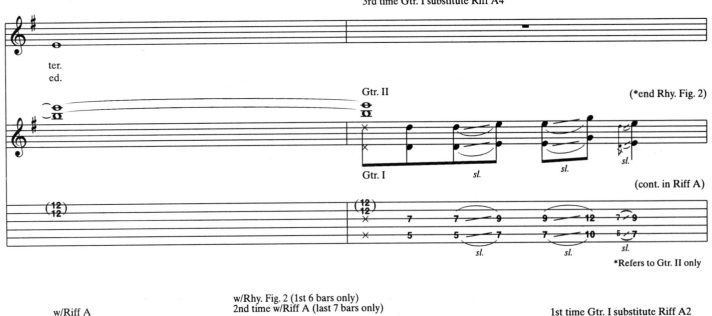

2nd time Gtr. I substitute Riff A3
3rd time Gtr. I substitute Riff A4

Gtr. II

(*end Rhy. Fig. 2)

Gtr. I

(cont. in Riff A)

ter.
ed.

*Refers to Gtr. II only

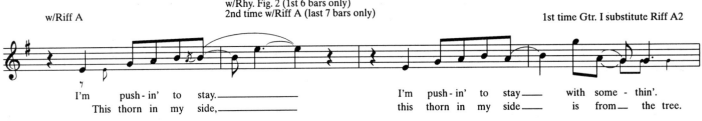

w/Riff A

w/Rhy. Fig. 2 (1st 6 bars only)
2nd time w/Riff A (last 7 bars only)

1st time Gtr. I substitute Riff A2

I'm push-in' to stay._____
This thorn in my side,_____

I'm push-in' to stay___ with some-thin'.
this thorn in my side___ is from___ the tree.

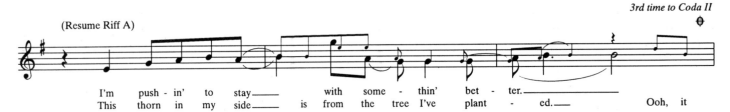

(Resume Riff A)

3rd time to Coda II

I'm push-in' to stay___ with some-thin' bet-ter._____
This thorn in my side___ is from the tree I've plant-ed.___

Ooh, it

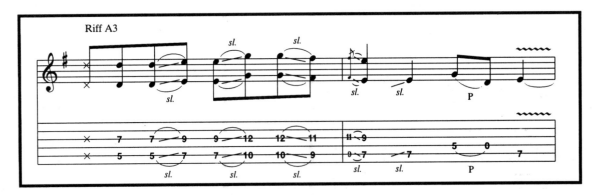

Riff A3

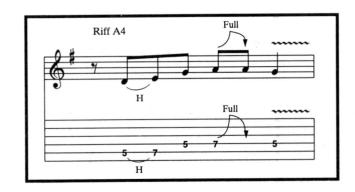

Riff A4

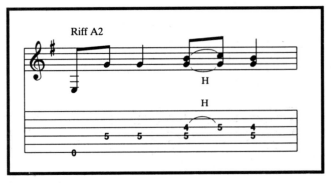

Riff A2

The bleed - ing of me.

84

(end half time feel)

Ooh,_____ come on,_____ ba - by.

w/Rhy. Fig. 5 (Gtrs. I & II)

w/Rhy. Fig. 5A (3 times)

trem. pick

CURE

Words and Music by
James Hetfield and Lars Ulrich

Tune down 1/2 step:
⑥=E♭ ③=G♭
⑤=A♭ ②=B♭
④=D♭ ①=E♭

Moderate Rock ♩ = 120

Intro (Drums)   Gtr. I   Rhy. Fig. 1 ___   (end Rhy. Fig. 1)

1st Verse
w/Rhy. Fig. 1 (7½ times)

(Spoken:) The man takes another bullet.   He keeps them all within.

He must seek no matter how it hurts,

so don't fool again.   Yeah. _____   *He thinks the an-swer's cold_
*Doubled by spoken voice (next 7 bars only)

___ and in his hand.   He takes his___ med-i-cine. _

The man takes an-oth-er bul-let.   Yeah,___ he's been fooled a-gain._

Un-cross your arms,   take and throw 'em to the cure,   say,

Rhy. Fill 1
Gtr. I   Gtrs. I & II   (end Rhy. Fill 1)

P.M. ------------*-------------

*Gradually release P.M.

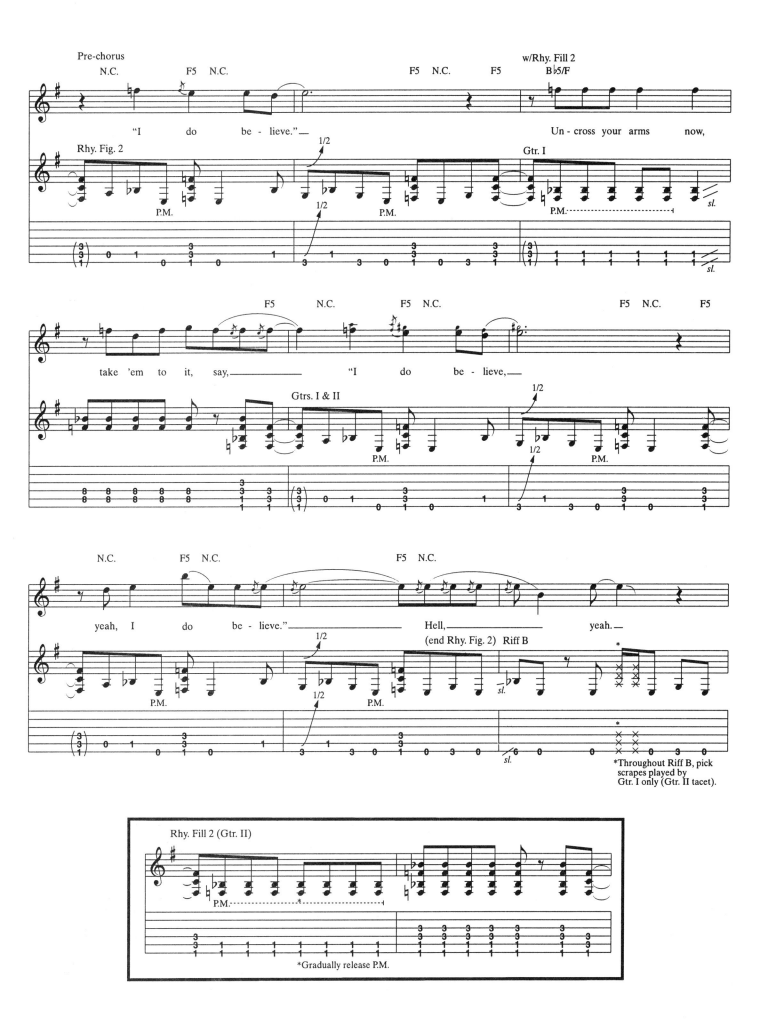

*With one of gtr.'s vol. knobs set to zero,
flick toggle switch back and forth in rhythm indicated.
(Rhythm shown is for "on" position only.)

**Both stgs. caught and
bent w/L.H. ring finger

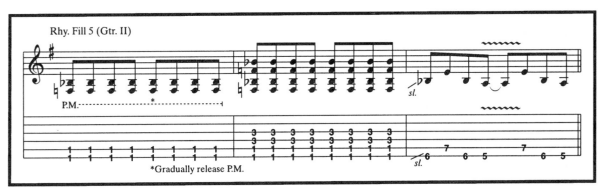

*Gradually release P.M.

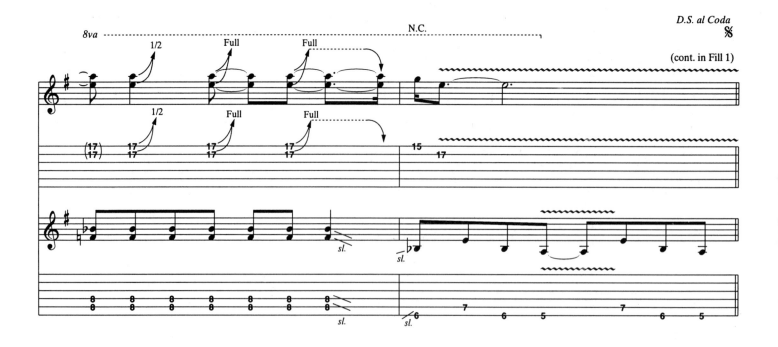

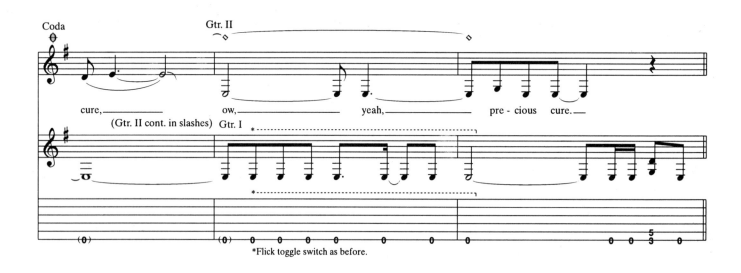

*Flick toggle switch as before.

I do be-lieve.___ I do be-lieve. I do be-lieve, I do be-lieve, I do be-lieve.___

Gtrs. I & II

Chorus / Outro
w/Rhy. Fig. 3 (1st 2 bars only) (Gtr. I: 4 times; Gtr. II: 3½ times)

N.C. E5   N.C.   E5

___ Bet - ting on___ the cure.___ Yeah, it

N.C.   E5   N.C.   E5

must get bet-ter than this.___ Need to feel se-cure.___ Yeah, it's

w/Rhy. Fig. 3 (Gtr. I)
N.C.   E5   N.C.

got-ta get bet-ter than this,___ this,___ yeah.___

Gtr. II

E5   N.C.   E5

___ It must get bet - ter than this.___

POOR TWISTED ME

Words and Music by
James Hetfield and Lars Ulrich

*Striking muffled stgs.
sometimes causes random
harmonics to sound (next 5 bars).

1st, 2nd Verses
N.C.(A5)

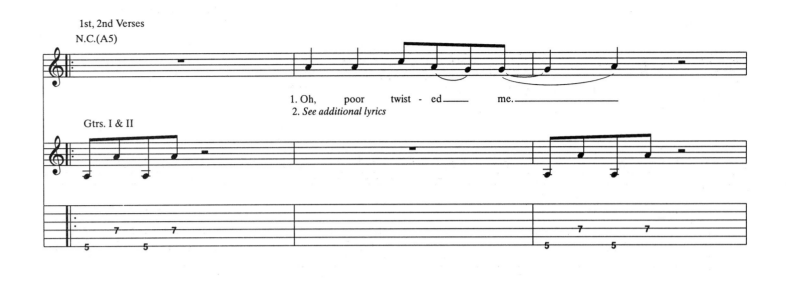

1. Oh, poor twist - ed____ me.____
2. *See additional lyrics*

Gtrs. I & II

Oh, poor twist - ed me.____

Gtrs. I & II

I

(Gtr. II out)

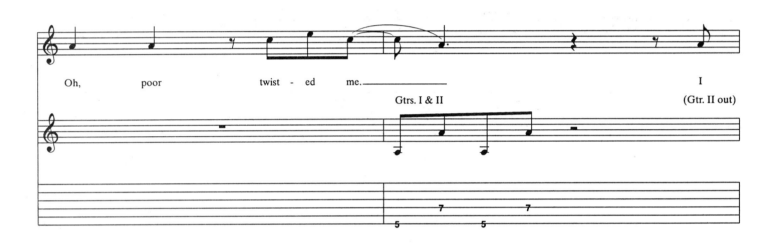

G5

feast on sym - pa - thy.____ I chew____ on suf - fer.____

Gtr. III

dist. tone
w/slide

Gtr. I

sl.

sl.

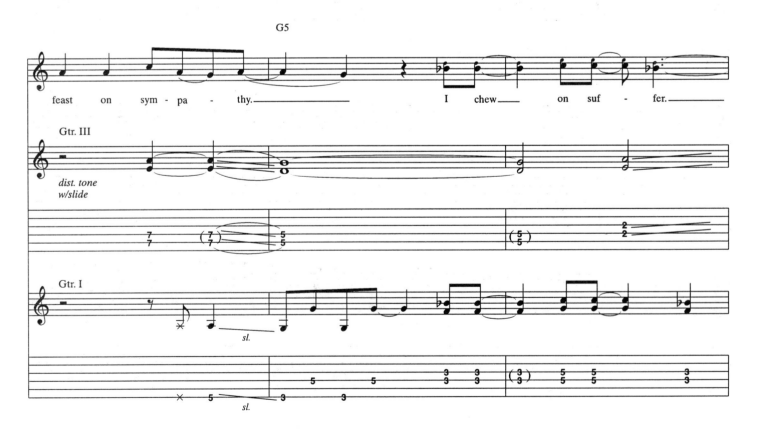

102

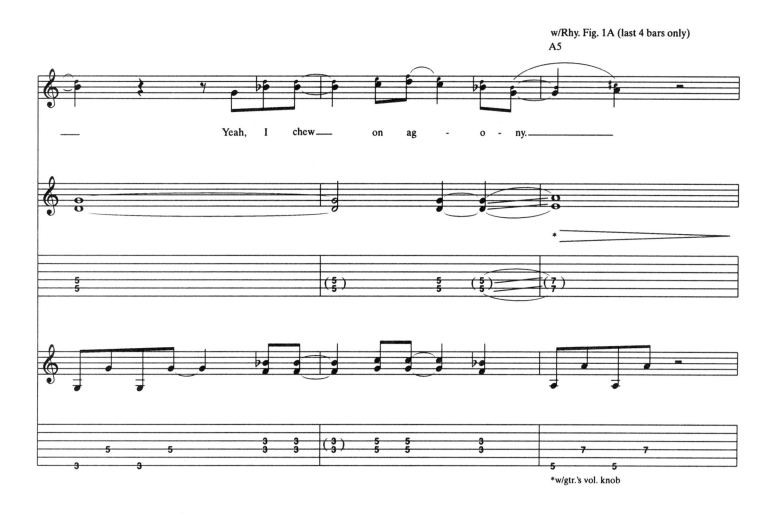

Yeah, I chew— on ag - o - ny.—

*w/gtr.'s vol. knob

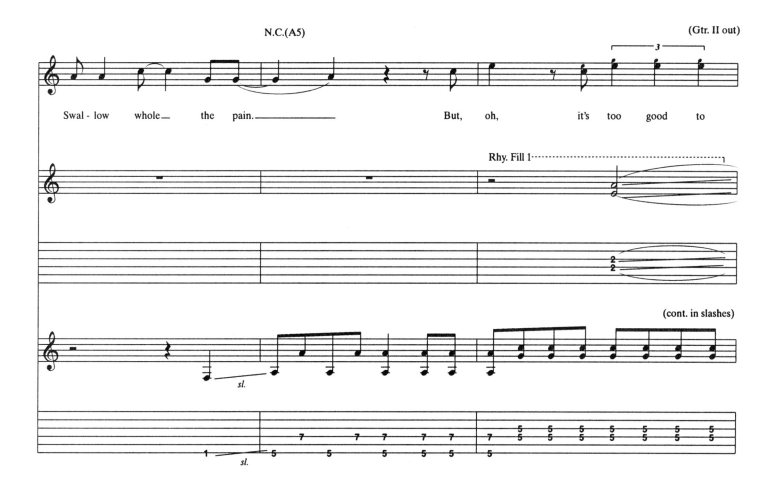

N.C.(A5)   (Gtr. II out)

Swal - low whole— the pain.— But, oh, it's too good to

Rhy. Fill 1

(cont. in slashes)

be _____ that all this___ mis - er - y, _____ just for,

oh, poor twist - ed me. _____

Ooh, yeah.

Poor twist - ed me. _____

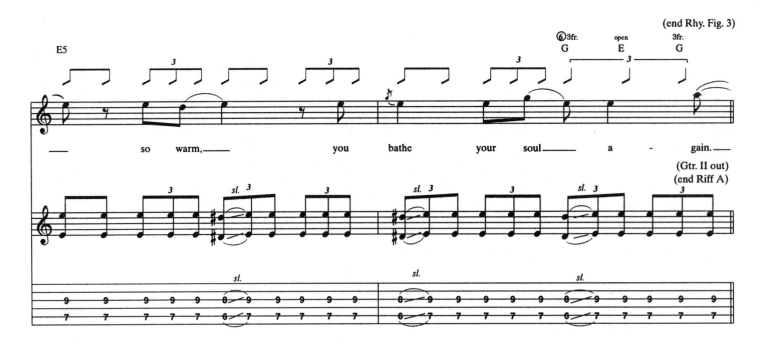

Half time feel
Guitar solo
w/*Rhy. Fig. 1 (1st 6 bars only)

*w/slight variations ad lib

Additional Lyrics

2. Poor mistreated me
   Poor mistreated me.
   I drown without a sea.
   Lungs filled with sorrow,
   Lungs filled with misery.
   Inhaling the deep, dark blue.
   Woe, woe is me.
   Such a burden to be
   The poor mistreated me, yeah.

WASTING MY HATE

Words and Music by James Hetfield,
Lars Ulrich and Kirk Hammett

and I won't waste — my hate — on you. —

*Throughout verses, bass plays E when gtr. plays F5.

and I won't waste— my hate— on you,—

Gtrs. I & II

2nd time to Coda I;
3rd time to Coda II

(end half time feel)

waste my hate— on— you.— Hate!

(3rd time Gtr. I cont. in slashes)

w/*Riff B (Gtrs. I & II)
N.C.

G5   A5   N.C. G5 A5   N.C.

*Last note is not tied.

G5   A5   N.C. G5 A5   N.C.

Ha, ha.

2nd Verse
w/*Rhy. Fig. 1
E5   F5   E5

Think you're worth—y now?—   You think e-nough to e-

*Gtr. II plays 1st 7 bars only.

F5   E5   F5   A D5 E5

ven raise— the brow— and to laugh and tip— that two-pr-onged—

114

116

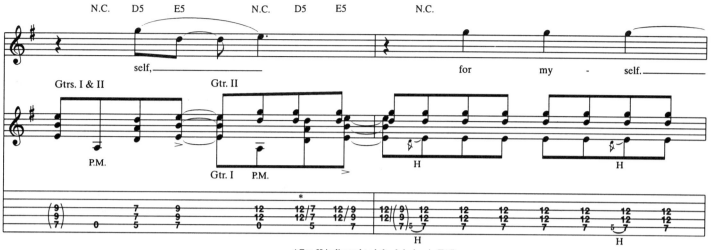

*Gtr. II indicated to left of slashes in TAB.

MAMA SAID

Words and Music by
James Hetfield and Lars Ulrich

Tune down 1/2 step:
⑥=E♭ ③=G♭
⑤=A♭ ②=B♭
④=D♭ ①=E♭

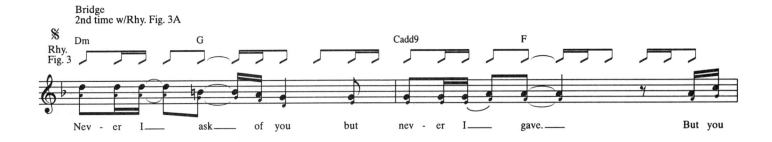

Bridge
2nd time w/Rhy. Fig. 3A

Rhy. Fig. 3

Dm　　　　　　　　　G　　　　　　　　　　　Cadd9　　　　　　F

Nev - er I__ ask__ of you　but　nev - er I__ gave.__　　　But you

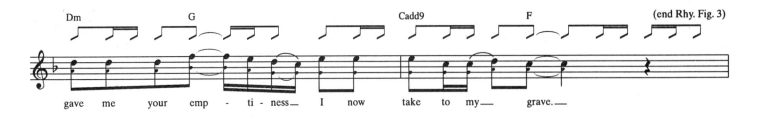

Dm　　　　　　　　　G　　　　　　　　　　　Cadd9　　　　　　F　　　(end Rhy. Fig. 3)

gave　me　your　emp - ti - ness__　I　now　take　to my__　grave.__

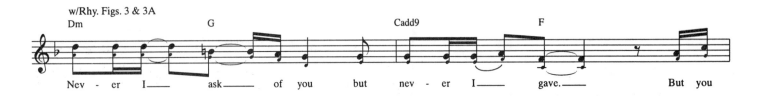

w/Rhy. Figs. 3 & 3A

Dm　　　　　　　　　G　　　　　　　　　　　Cadd9　　　　　　F

Nev - er I__ ask__ of you　but　nev - er I__　gave.__　　　But you

Dm　　　　　　　　　G　　　　　　　　　　　Cadd9　　　　　　F　　　*To Coda* ⊕

gave　me　your　emp - ti - ness__　I　now　take__ to my__　grave.__　　　So

Dm　Cadd9　Bb　G　　Am　　Asus4　　　　　　　3rd Verse
　　　　　　　　　　　　　　　　　　　　　w/Rhy. Fig. 1 (1¾ times)
Gtr. I　　　　　　　　　　　　　　　　　　　Dm

let　this　heart　be__　still.__　　　　　　　Ma - ma,　now__ I'm com - ing__ home,　I'm not

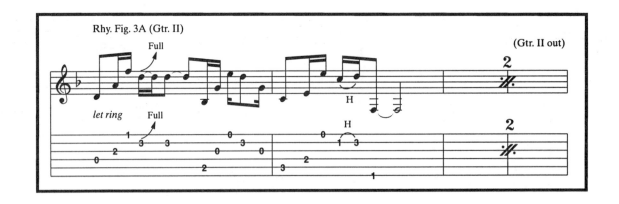

Rhy. Fig. 3A (Gtr. II)

(Gtr. II out)

Full

let ring　Full　　　　　　　　　　　H

all you wished of me.____ A moth-er's love_ for her_ son,_ un - spo-ken, help me be._____ Yeah, I

Gtr. II

w/wah as filter

took your love_ for grant - ed, and all the things you said to me,_____ yeah._____ I
(...things you said to me.)

need_ your arms_ to wel - come me, but a cold stone's all I see._____

(Gtr. II out)

(wah off)

Chorus
w/Rhy. Fig. 2 (last 6 bars only) & *Fill 1

Let my___ heart go.____ Let your___ son

*Last note is tied.
w/slight variations ad lib

grow._____ Ma - ma, let my__ heart go,_____ or

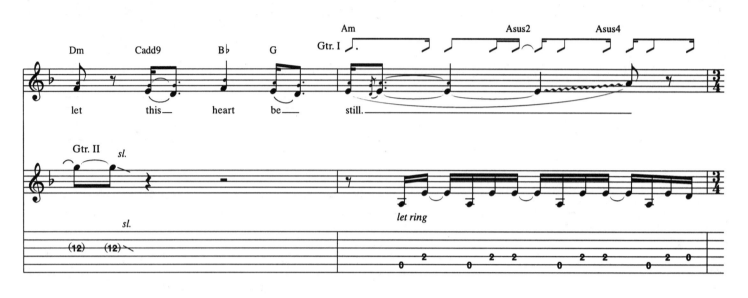

let this__ heart be__ still.

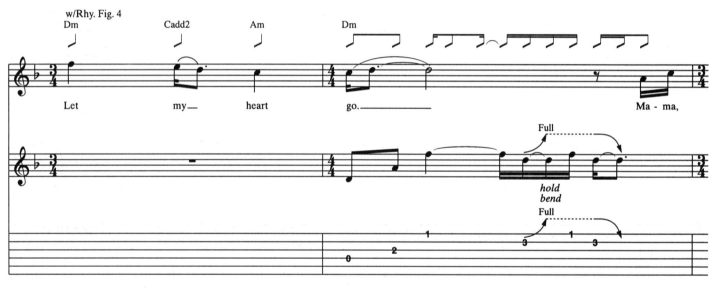

Let my__ heart go._____ Ma - ma,

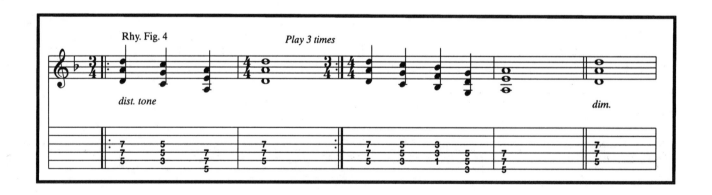

THORN WITHIN

Words and Music by James Hetfield,
Lars Ulrich and Kirk Hammett

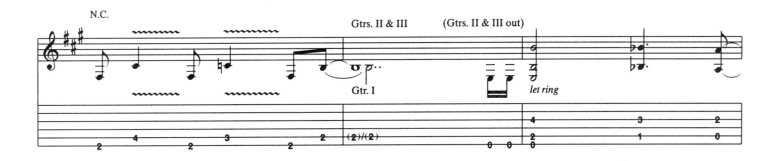

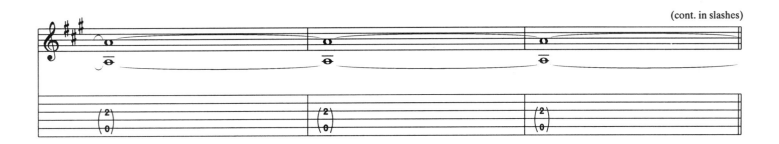

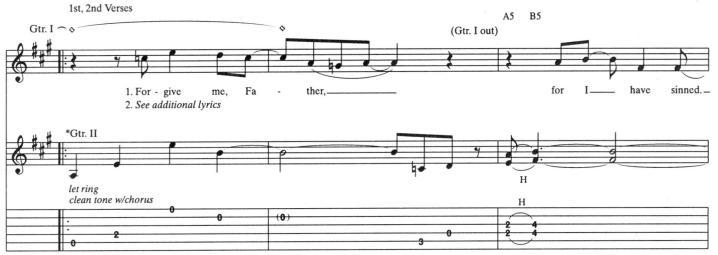

*During 2nd Verse, play all parts w/slight variations ad lib.

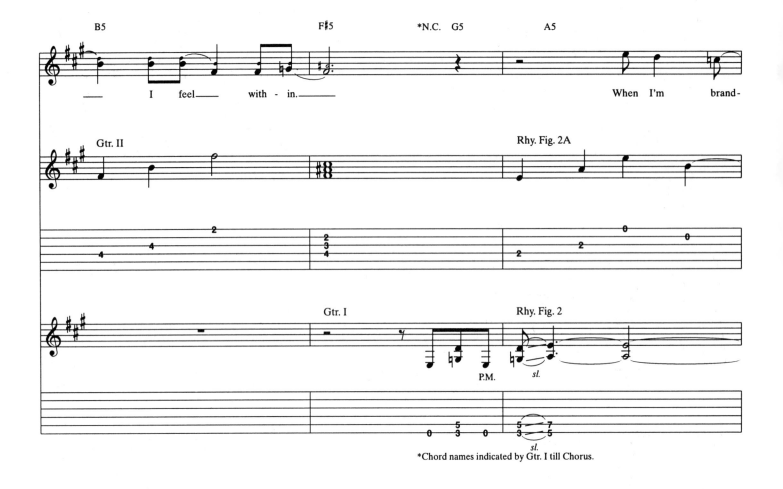

*Chord names indicated by Gtr. I till Chorus.

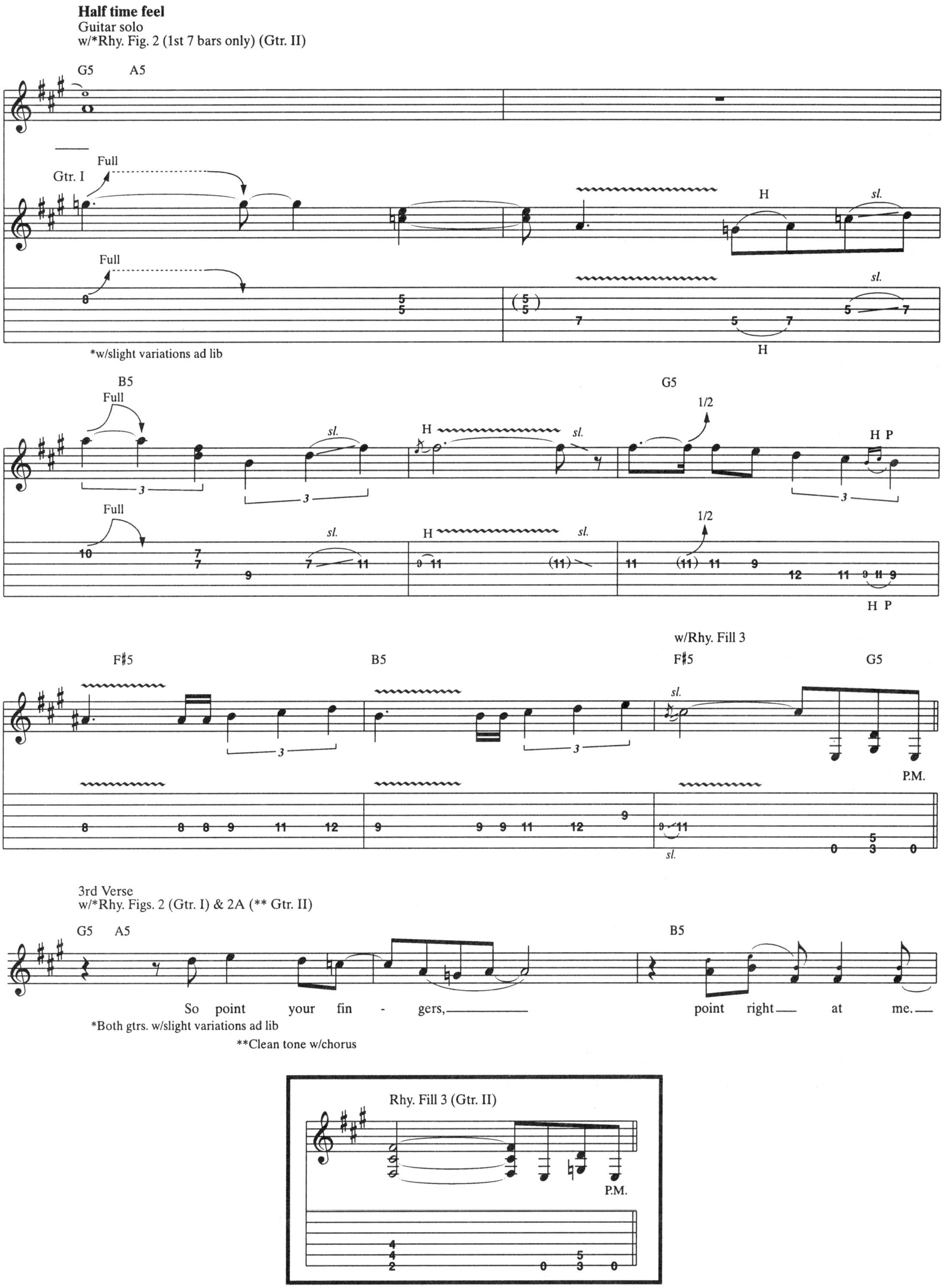
Half time feel
Guitar solo
w/*Rhy. Fig. 2 (1st 7 bars only) (Gtr. II)
G5 A5
Gtr. I
Full
H
sl.
*w/slight variations ad lib
B5
G5
1/2
H P
F♯5
w/Rhy. Fill 3
P.M.
3rd Verse
w/*Rhy. Figs. 2 (Gtr. I) & 2A (** Gtr. II)
So point your fin - gers,
point right at me.
*Both gtrs. w/slight variations ad lib
**Clean tone w/chorus
Rhy. Fill 3 (Gtr. II)

133

I am the thorn with-in.

Additional Lyrics

2. Forgive me, Father, for I have sinned.
   Find me guilty when true guilt is from within.
   So point your fingers, point right at me.
   For I am shadows and will follow you.
   One and the same are we. *(To Chorus)*

RONNIE

Words and Music by
James Hetfield and Lars Ulrich

135

1st Verse

Sto - ry starts,— qui - et town.— Small town boy,— big— time frown.—

Nev - er talks,— nev - er plays.— Dif - f'rent path,— lost his— way.—

streets of red,— red I'm a-fraid.— There's no con-fet-ti, no pa-rade.— Noth-

ing hap-pens in this bor-ing place,— but, oh my God,— how it all— did change.. Now they

all pray,— blood stain wash a-way.—

141

w/Rhy. Fill 3

we all know why the children called him "Ronnie Frown". When he

pulled that gun from his pocket, and they all fall down,___ down,___ down.___

Chorus
w/Rhy. Figs. 1 & 1A
N.C.(A)

w/Rhy. Fill 2 (1st bar only)
C5   D5   C5

___ He said, "Lost my way___ this blood-y day.___ Lost my___ way."___ Yeah,─ yeah, I heard him.

w/Rhy. Figs. 1 (1st 3 bars only) & 1A
N.C.(A)

He screamed, "Lost my way___ this blood-y day.___ Lost my___ way."___

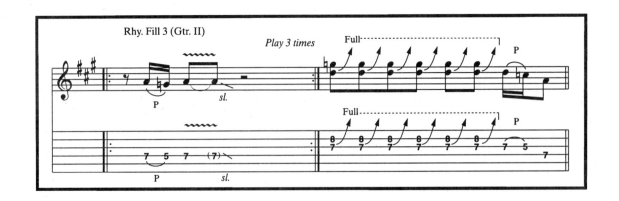

Rhy. Fill 3 (Gtr. II)

Play 3 times

142

THE OUTLAW TORN

Words and Music by
James Hetfield and Lars Ulrich

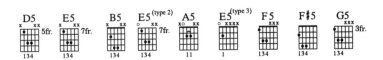

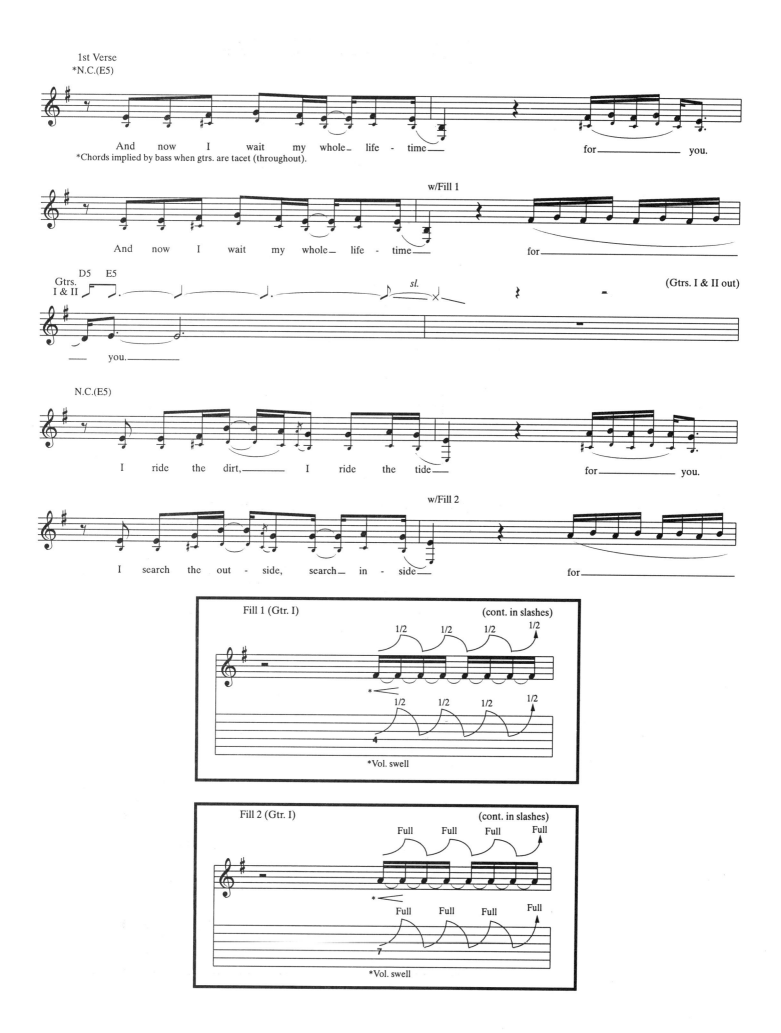

151

To find out what's up in the world of Metallica, check out the Metallica Club: the worldwide fan club that's completely guided, controlled and overseen by the band. Send a self-addressed stamped envelope to:

The Metallica Club
P.O. Box 18327
Knoxville, TN 37928-2327
(from outside the United States, please include an International Response Coupon)

Or e-mail your full name and address to:

METCLUB@aol.com
Metallica Worldwide Web Address:
http://www.metclub.com

• TABLATURE EXPLANATION/NOTATION LEGEND •

TABLATURE: A six-line staff that graphically represents the guitar fingerboard. By placing a number on the appropriate line, the string and fret of any note can be indicated. For example:

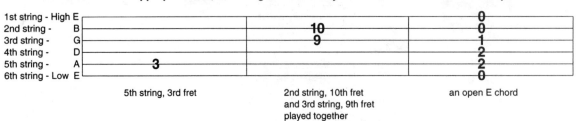

| 1st string - High E |
| 2nd string - B |
| 3rd string - G |
| 4th string - D |
| 5th string - A |
| 6th string - Low E |

5th string, 3rd fret   2nd string, 10th fret and 3rd string, 9th fret played together   an open E chord

Definitions for Special Guitar Notation

BEND: Strike the note and bend up ½ step (one fret).

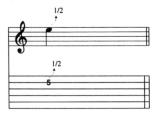

BEND: Strike the note and bend up a whole step (two frets).

BEND AND RELEASE: Strike the note and bend up ½ (or whole) step, then release the bend back to the original note. All three notes are tied; only the first note is struck.

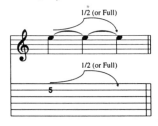

PRE-BEND: Bend the note up ½ (or whole) step, then strike it.

PRE-BEND AND RELEASE: Bend the note up ½ (or whole) step, strike it and release the bend back to the original note.

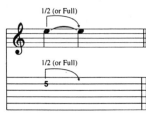

UNISON BEND: Strike the two notes simultaneously and bend the lower note to the pitch of the higher.

VIBRATO: Vibrate the note by rapidly bending and releasing the string with a left-hand finger.

WIDE OR EXAGGERATED VIBRATO: Vibrate the pitch to a greater degree with a left-hand finger or the tremolo bar.

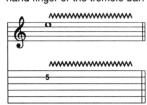

SLIDE: Strike the first note and then with the same left-hand finger move up the string to the second note. The second note is not struck.

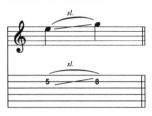

SLIDE: Same as above, except the second note is struck.

SLIDE: Slide up to the note indicated from a few frets below.

HAMMER-ON: Strike the first (lower) note, then sound the higher note with another finger by fretting it without picking.

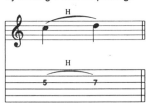

PULL-OFF: Place both fingers on the notes to be sounded. Strike the first (higher) note, then sound the lower note by pulling the finger off the higher note while keeping the lower note fretted.

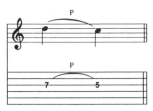

TRILL: Very rapidly alternate between the note indicated and the small note shown in parentheses by hammering on and pulling off.

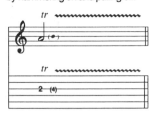

TAPPING: Hammer ("tap") the fret indicated with the right-hand index or middle finger and pull off to the note fretted by the left hand.

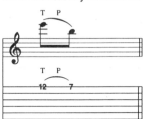

NATURAL HARMONIC: With a left-hand finger, lightly touch the string over the fret indicated, then strike it. A chime-like sound is produced.

ARTIFICIAL HARMONIC: Fret the note normally and sound the harmonic by adding the right-hand thumb edge or index finger tip to the normal pick attack.

A.H. pitch: E

TREMOLO BAR: Drop the note by the number of steps indicated, then return to original pitch.

PALM MUTE: With the right hand, partially mute the note by lightly touching the string just before the bridge.

MUFFLED STRINGS: Lay the left hand across the strings without depressing them to the fret-board; strike the strings with the right hand, producing a percussive sound.

PICK SLIDE: Rub the pick edge down the length of the string to produce a scratchy sound.

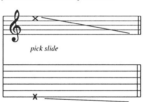

TREMOLO PICKING: Pick the note as rapidly and continuously as possible.

RHYTHM SLASHES: Strum chords in rhythm indicated. Use chord voicings found in the fingering diagrams at the top of the first page of the transcription.

SINGLE-NOTE RHYTHM SLASHES: The circled number above the note name indicates which string to play. When successive notes are played on the same string, only the fret numbers are given.

Definitions of Musical Symbols

Symbol	Definition
8va	•Play an octave higher than written
15ma	•Play two octaves higher than written
loco	•Play as written
pp (pianissimo)	•Very soft
p (piano)	•Soft
mp (mezzo-piano)	•Moderately soft
mf (mezzo-forte)	•Moderately loud
f (forte)	•Loud
ff (fortissimo)	•Very Loud
(accent)	•Accentuate note (play it louder)
(accent)	•Accentuate note with great intensity
(staccato)	•Play note short
(mark)	•Repeat previous beat (used for quarter or eighth notes)
(mark)	•Repeat previous beat (used for sixteenth notes)
∕.	•Repeat previous measure
‖: :‖	• Repeat measures between repeat signs
‖: 1. : 2. ‖	•When a repeated section has different endings, play the first ending only the first time and the second ending only the second time.
D.S. al Coda	•Go back to the sign (%) and play to the measure marked "To Coda," then skip to the section labeled "Coda."
D.C. al Fine	•Go back to the beginning of the song and play until the measue marked "Fine" (end).